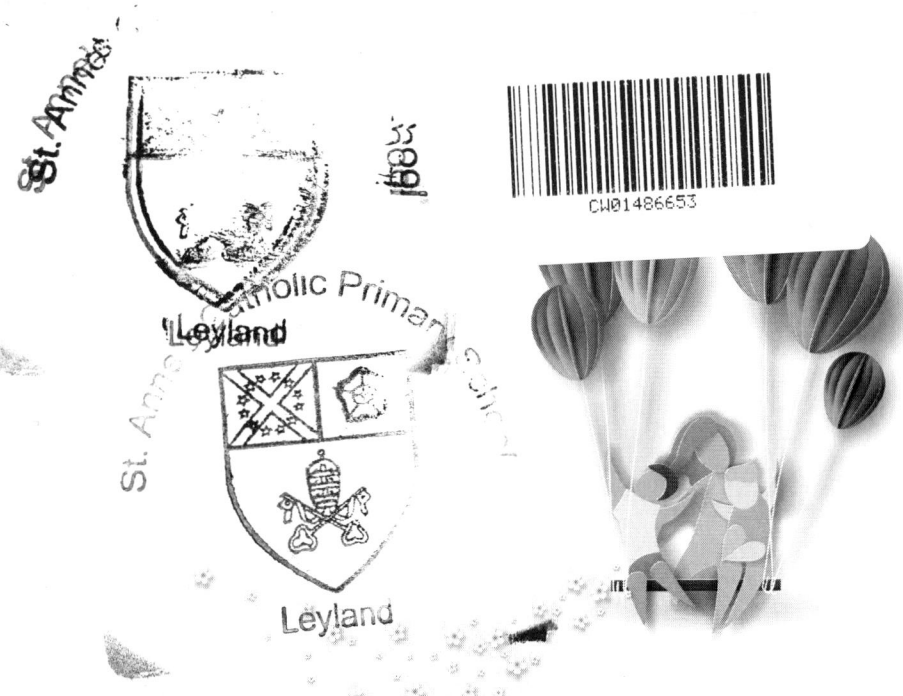

World's Best Mum
Heartfelt Words

Edited by Jenni Harrison

First published in Great Britain in 2019 by:

 Young**Writers**

Young Writers
Remus House
Coltsfoot Drive
Peterborough
PE2 9BF
Telephone: 01733 890066
Website: www.youngwriters.co.uk

All Rights Reserved
Book Design by Ali Smith
© Copyright Contributors 2019
SB ISBN 978-1-78988-765-5
HB ISBN 978-1-83928-168-6

Printed and bound in the UK by BookPrintingUK
Website: www.bookprintinguk.com

Foreword

Here at Young Writers our defining aim
is to promote the joys of reading and writing to
children and young adults and we are committed to
nurturing the creative talents of the next generation.
By allowing them to see their own work in print we believe
their confidence and love of creative writing will grow.

We are proud to present this collection of poems, the
result of our latest competition 'World's Best Mum'.
Using poetry as a tool to express their appreciation and
admiration of all these things a mother does, these young
writers give personal dedications to the irreplaceable super
mum in their life. The selection process was a very difficult
task, yet the love and enthusiasm put into all of the entries
ensured that we enjoyed reading each and every one.

Including a medley of different voices and poetic styles,
such as rhyming verse and the acrostic, this is an endearing
anthology in which talented young writers use their creative
flow of words to give an important message to
their mum in a million: thank you.

Contents

The Poems

Mother Like No Other

Oh Mother, you are like no other,
Throughout the years, you've always been a wonderful
mother to see.
When I was small, you took the time,
To make me fly up high.

As I grew older, you were there
And you were the only one I could call.
I know that I could count on you,
You'd never let me fall.

So many hard times in my life
You've helped me get through.
Oh, what a wonderful mother,
You are just like no other.

Sam Golzar-Tehrani

Is My Mom An Alien?

Is my mum an alien?
She stays awake when we're asleep,
To keep away the ghouls and creeps.
She's up in the morning with breakfast all ready,
I doubt she even sleeps.
She can do many things at once,
Cooking, sweeping, washing up,
Does she have lots of hands and feet?
She drops us to school and is there at the gate.
At the end of the day,
She is never late.
We walk in the house and it is always neat,
Dinner on the table all ready to eat!
Everything is in order, she has no faults,
She makes me wonder...
Is my mum an alien?

My mum goes on missions
Up in the sky
Late at midnight,
With a flashing cry
She eats her supper all wrong,
She even licks the plates
Whilst listening to a terrible song.
This is how she normally is,
She puts my mind into a quiz.
All these things make me think,
That my mum is an alien,
But I still love her.

Ume-Habeebah Imran

My Awesome Mother

Mother, you make my day and never give up helping me,
You have a kind heart like no one else.
I will never stop loving you,
I am sure you will never stop loving me.

I'm so lucky to have you as my mum,
When I sleep, I think of you.
I may make you stressed,
But in my heart I will always love you.
You work very hard to raise me,
To be a well-mannered girl.

I hope this made you smile,
I hope you never forget this.

Stacey Kimani (8)

Mother

M um, you are always there for us.
O n most days you cook the dinner.
T he others, I do.
H ome is a good place, because you are there.
E very day you help those things too.*
R eally good does not describe you...
...because you are breathtaking and awe-inspiring.

Those things, otherwise known as twins.

Hannah Wotton

Sweetest Mum Ever

Mum is nice,
Mum is sweet,
I like her soft hugs,
Which make me smile.

Her hair is soft and blonde,
She has lush green eyes,
And a big great smile.

She also reads to me every night with delight,
I love her so much,
She is the best mum ever!

Galena Mihova (8)

I Love You, Mommy!

From the day my eyes fluttered open,
When your eyes beamed down like stars,
Eyes like gems from the depths of the ocean,
The hidden world you made ours.

From the day I first said your name,
To the moment I grasped your hand,
I knew I'd be safe beside you,
Like how broken shells still cling to the sand.

From the days when tears stream down my face,
To the hours when I'm no longer blue,
I know through all the days I've grown,
I've been standing next to you.

Madeleine Elizabeth Huffine

My Mum

My mum looks after me,
No matter how tough and annoying I can be.
She's barely under stress,
And she always creates times that are the best!
She makes me really happy,
But she gets angry when I get too snappy.
She cooks me food,
And she's rarely rude.
My mum's the best,
I'm the chick in her nest.
That's pretty hard to beat,
Unless you cheat!

Kelda-Emma Lauren-Owusu

Sunday Fun Day

Roses are red,
Violets are blue,
I would never have,
Another mum like you.

You're the most exquisite,
You're the best,
So happy Mother's Day,
To the best mum in the world.
PS You cannot fool this lady.

Junior Mbaru

Nice Life

Apples are red,
Blueberries are blue,
Wait! This isn't about fruit,
This is about you!

You're the best,
Kind too.
I just can't stop thinking about you!

The only thing,
I want to say,
Is...

Happy Mother's Day!

Daniella Mbaru

My Mummy, My Hero

Mummy, Mummy, Mummy,
I love you,
I am your day and night,
When I am ill you get a fright.

Mummy, Mummy, Mummy,
I love you,
You cook tasty food,
When you are in a good mood.

Mummy, Mummy, Mummy,
I love you,
You are beautiful
And lovely too!

Mummy, Mummy, Mummy
I love you,
You take me to school
And you take me to the swimming pool.

Mummy, Mummy, Mummy
I love you,
You are the best
Better than the rest!

Amelia Ahmad

My Passionate Mum

My passionate mum,
Looked after me since I was sucking my thumb.
For she is a luscious mother to me,
She is the best mother you could have, you see.
Mum is so nice, you can tell,
How she treats me so entirely well.
I love my mum so,
Because she's nice to me every day, even tomorrow.
She is so ardent and kind,
She can read my mind.

Nihara Dumbukola

Poem For Mother's Day

M ost people may love you but Mother loves you more.
O ther people may not care but Mother will always care.
T hey always support you and love you no matter what they say to you.
H er love is unconditional for her children.
E verything is important to tell your mum.
R eal love comes from good, beautiful, generous, smart, intelligent mums like my mum.

Tidankay Abiba Doukoure

Mother's Day

Mum, Mother, Mom,
Whatever you may be called I will love you

Forever and forever it will be,
I thought of buying you chocolates

But I knew you would prefer
A forever bouquet from your favourite daughter.

Megan Mcintyre

My Mother, The Best!

Everyone says their mother is the best,
But that is not true 'cause I'm the lucky one,
The world's best mother belongs to me.

To the best mother in the world,
You are an angel in disguise.
I never have to ask for your help,
You are always there to guide me.

You've been my rock throughout my life,
Wanting nothing in return.
You've made me who I am today,
Helping me grow and learn.

Thank you will never be enough,
For everything.
You're my friend, my counsellor,
My guardian angel,
But most importantly,
My mum.

Jasleen Kaur (13)

World's Best Mum

H appy Mother's Day
A ll the support you have given me,
P ast and
P resent,
Y ou have helped me through all of my life.

M um, I am so proud to be your son,
O ther people don't have a mum like you,
T hat's why I am thankful that you're here.
H appy endings don't always happen, but this will be one.
E very day you help me in some way,
R arely people are like you,
S o that's why I want to say happy Mother's Day to you.

D ay and night you are there for me,
A nd I love you,
Y ou are the best.

Patrik Kocz (10)

Irreplaceable

A mother like mine is irreplaceable:
Eyes that brightly shine forever
That say we'll always laugh together
Perfect's too weak a word
Arms are always open wide
To tightly hold me by her side
Perfect's too weak a word
Whatever problem, great or small
She's never further than a call
To lift me up when down I fall
She knows precisely how to say
"I love you more and more each day"
And perfect's too weak a word.

A mother like mine is irreplaceable:
Her laugh enchanting every word
When she teases, calling me absurd
Perfect's too weak a word
When tears are leaking down my cheeks
She always comfortingly speaks
Perfect's too weak a word
Doesn't matter what we do
The bond is strong between us two
Making memories, glimmering new
"I love you" is nowhere near a quarter
Of what it means to be your daughter
And perfect's too weak a word.

Emma Huntingford

My Mum Is Nice

My mum is nice.
My mum is super and very good,
I love her very much.
She is beautiful.
I really, really love her.
My mum is so, so, so good.
My mum is very good.
She is having a cup of tea.
Mum is so good.
She is really good and I love her!

Elizabeth White

A Hundred Moons For You

A hundred moons can't give the light you emit,
Nor can a thousand suns equate to your warmth.
For flowers bloom only in your command,
And it's by your signal, the birds fly out at dawn.

If your compassion could be put into words,
Then the volumes would go on and on.
If your kindness was put into a melody,
The symphony would be an infinite song.

Your everyday battles to make us content,
Can never be praised enough.
Amongst the greys of flocking birds,
You're the only angelical dove.

You're the definition of a mother,
And amongst pearls and emeralds, you should have a seat,
As an ordinary throne isn't worthy of you,
As paradise lies beneath your feet.

Nuha, Hiba & Yumna Anoosdeen

To The Strongest Woman I Will Ever Know

To the strongest woman I will ever know.
At first glance Mom's hands may seem crippled and meek.
She flinches when you bump them and her grip is quite weak.
But these hands are a reflection of the woman inside,
Although burdened with limits, still strong with pride.
When opening a jar seems too great a task,
It's only after great hesitation that she finally asks.
Don't let that mislead you for you must understand,
It's not what they can't do, but rather what they can.
These hands have the strength to raise a family right,
To wipe away every tear and hold you real tight.
They come together each day in prayer,
And whenever you need them, they're always right there.
So if these hands don't appear all that tough,
Remember they're full of tenderness and love
And for me that's enough.

Ayesha Ameer

Queen Of Mums

My mum is the special one
The only one I need for me.
Her heart is full of love
The only thing I see.
The best thing I like about her
Is when she always has my back for whatever I do.
The thing is, we stick to each other like goo.
She is a lifesaver to me.

Isabel John

Mother's Love...

My mum is an absolute queen,
Who loves everything to be clean.
However, her bossiness is quite extreme,
Which makes her quite mean.

Her heart is one of a kind,
Like her thoughts in her mind.
Raging like the storm,
Yet can be soothing like the ocean.

Mum is a word,
A word we've all heard.
Yet no one had really known,
As soon as you are grown,
That you will miss the warmth,
Of your lovely mother's arms.

Faye Lok Fei Chan

World's Best Mum

For all the times that I forgot to say thank you,
For all the special little things you do for me,
For all the words that sometimes go unspoken,
I need to say, you are the best and mean it, I really do.

You are the best, because of the way you listen,
And for kind support throughout the past twelve years,
And for teaching me the meaning of compassion and love,
And sharing in my triumphs and my tears.

And, if at times I might seem ungrateful,
I want to say, I truly hope you see,
That nothing you have done has been forgotten,
And day by day you just mean more and more to me.

Thank you for being here!

Jasmin Saini

Our Mother

Our mother is wonderful, our mother is kind,
Our mother is the best person on Earth combined.
She can do tricks, like pick up sticks,
She can climb a tree, swing and say, "Whoopee!"

But what is weird is that she doesn't like certain meals;
What she eats instead is half of my bed.

She likes to eat objects - god knows why.
She likes to eat them, even a fly.
Half of my book is gone right now,
Half of my hairband, half of my crown!

But even though our mother is weird,
I still love her from ear to ear.

Niamh Amanpreet Affley

My Mum Does Everything Wrong

My mum does everything wrong,
She dresses me in summer clothes in the winter
And winter clothes in the summer.
She puts a toy in my baby brother's mouth instead of a dummy,
And thinks that is so funny!

She makes me do homework in the holidays,
And takes me on trips on regular school days.
My mum does everything wrong.
At least that's what I say to my teachers,
When I answer that 1 and 1 make 11.

Sean Kirpal Affley

Beloved Mummy

Mum, you are amazing,
You have no idea you are beloved,
Mummy, you care,
No stare,
Not even a glare,
All you do is care,
All you do is care.

You're the best,
You make me calm when I'm stressed,
Oh, Mummy, you're the best.
You let me play,
You let my friend stay,
And buy me my favourite toy,
Oh, Mummy, you really are the best.

Aish Sarmad

Special Is What You Are

Mums are amazing,
Mums are kind,
Mums are wonderful,
Why is this?

Some people say a mum is a mum.
But they are more than that!

Mums are lifesavers!
They are what make you special,
Think what your mum does to you,
What could you do to her?

Your mum is the only reason you are here,
Think how happy your mum was when you were born.
What could you do this Mother's Day,
To make your mum know how special she is?

Jaanavi Kalsi (10)

World's Best Mum

Oh Mummy, oh dearest Mummy,
I have loved you since I was born.
I've never seen you upset or angry with me,
That's why you're my favourite.

Oh Mummy, oh dearest Mummy,
You've always shown me care.
That is why I try to do the same for you,
That is why I have written this poem,
To tell you how much I love you.

Lily Shipley

To You: Mum

The first word we said was
"Ma Ma"
Before we could even walk, we called out your name.
Before we entered primary school, we called out your name.
When we had a hard decision to make, we asked you.
We called out your name.
"Mum"
When Dad left us, we were all afraid.
Even when life was tough, you stayed.
Every day you woke up at 6, just to hop on a train.
Every day you came for us, even in the rain.
When no one was there, you were!
You still stayed.
"Mummy"
You went through hell for us.
With no car, you took us on the bus.
With no husband, you had to play two roles.
You know you could have abandoned us,
But you didn't, you stayed.
 "Ma"
Because of your blood, sweat and tears,
We can accomplish our dreams.
Watch us, we promise your effort will not go to waste.
You suffered for us.
You cried for us.
We will be successful for you and make you proud.
Thank you, Mum, for everything you have done for us.
Our love for you is an endless tunnel.
Happy Mother's Day, Ma!

Damilola Ilori

Be Magnificent

Mums are magnificent
they do lots of chores
they find their way through mad mayhem
and put your clothes away in your newly-made drawers.
If you are ever sad, they come and make you glad
Mum's medicine treats those nasty bugs, but
the best things mums are good at are homely hugs.

Niamh Sabelle Burl Holland

A Mother Like No Other

Who is my mother?
Well, she's like no other!
The very reason I am here today!
She brightens me when I am feeling grey.

The most important person in my life!
Unlike a grandma, unlike a wife.
Not my brother, not my dad;
She's the one who makes me glad.

Not a sister or my cuz,
It's my mum that always does.
Mention anyone else now,
No one compares, Mum's the "WOW!"

The look you see in her eyes,
Tells a different story every time.
If she's sad, you feel her pain,
Her emotions are a contagious chain.

The expressions on her busy face,
Tell you she's always on the case.
There's always something on her mind,
But astonishingly, she's never behind.

She is the petal on a beautiful flower,
Emitting her radiance of immense power.
Of course, we know her as The Leader.
And I am sure, I will always need her.

She's the one to always help out,
She never wastes time faffing about.

She's always looking to make my life great.
And in addition, she's also a mate!

My mother does whatever is right,
And in an argument, she'll win the fight.
She's the supreme being of all time,
She is at the top of prime's prime.

Aaryan Thomas-Michael Manarkattu (11)

Nanny Shirley, The First Time I Saw You

The first time I saw you
You were so sweet and calm
I loved your smile and I still do now
But you're not around
I have looked high and low
To try and find you
But you're nowhere
I really miss you
I really do so I just wanted to say I love you!

Brooke Carter

She's My Mum

She's the ring in space around Saturn,
She's the centre of a floral pattern.

She's the soft sway of a snowflake,
She's the lovely lotus in a lake.

She's the diamond in a ring,
She's the queen of bling.

She has tremendous grace,
She reflects moonlight in her soft face.

She's the fizz in lemonade,
She's the sweetest cake of the highest grade.

She's the leader of the lions,
She's my mum.

Rohun Manarkattu

World's Best Mum

My mummy
always feeds my tummy
trying to make the food very yummy.
Sometimes she may get cross
but she still acts like a good boss.
Before I go to bed at night
my mum always hugs me tight.
When I feel sickly
my mum tries to get me better quickly.
My mum may not be a queen that's royal
but she is a queen that's loyal.
My mum is a star
better than the one above Mars
and when it is Mother's Day
I'll shout hip hip hooray!

Oluwatoni Iyiola-Ojo

World's Best Mum

Mum, Mum, Mum.
My dear mum.
I love you so much, Mum.

You always take care of me.
Every day you make food for me.

Mum, Mum, Mum.
I love you so much, Mum.

You are so kind and helpful, Mum.
You are the best mum in the world.

Mum, Mum, Mum.
I love you so much, Mum.

You always do too much for me, Mum,
You help me do my homework.
You made me a superstar in my school.

Mum, Mum, Mum.
I love you so much, Mum.

When you are not around, Mum,
I miss you so much, Mum.

Mum, Mum, Mum.
I love you so much, Mum.

Mobeen Yasin

Mummy's Beautiful Love

Mummy cooks our delicious family meals every day
She lets me get whatever toys I want so I can play
My mummy treats me with my favourite bubblegum ice cream without my say
She gives me lots of cuddles when I am ill to take the pain away
Sometimes Mummy takes me to the park and for a while we stay
Mummy teaches me how to be good and I hope she will be with me forever - for this I pray
Me and my little sister, Aria, love Mummy so much!
Thank you, Mummy, for your beautiful love and everything you do for our family.

Jasmin Sehdev

I Love You, Mummy

I ntrigued was she, appeared a shimmering star,

L ittle did she know, it was spectacular!
O ver the moon, appeared blissful moonlight,
V ery precious just like that glistening starlight.
E very day is full of your everlasting love,

Y ou and I shared wishes together from the shooting stars above,
O lder I get... the closer I am with you,
U nderstanding how much a loving mother can sacrifice like you,

M y eyes shed tears from all the beautiful memories we have made together, that will forever remain,
U s are like best friends, as you are always the shining sun that brightens my days over and over again.
M um, I love you!
M um, I want to let you know that I will forever be your little girl!
Y ou are so valuable to me, you are like the stars and galaxies!

Venus Lok Lokk Chan

World's Best Mummy

B est mummy is called Clare Georgy,
E verything she does with us is special,
S he makes everyone smile,
T hank you for being the best mummy.

M akes life amazing,
U nique personality (a very good one),
M arvellous hugs,
M akes the world a better place,
Y et still gives me and my brother lots of attention.

I love you, Mummy, and thank you for everything,
You make me smile,
And because you are in it the world is a nicer place.

Ethan Georgy

My Mum

My mum is so beautiful,
She is also very helpful.

She is so cuddly,
She is so lovely.

It makes me dream very well,
She must feel like a mermaid.

Emily Wotton

My Majestic Mother

My mum is never rude,
She always has a positive attitude.
My mum is very kind to me,
And she serves me tea.

My mum takes much care,
Also, she is often willing to share.
My mother is always there for me,
Even when times get scary.

Whenever I have a frown,
She tries to turn it upside down.

Ameerah Raza

My Mummy Is The Best

My mummy is the best,
When I am ill, you make me sit down and rest.
You do all the washing, cleaning and shopping.
All because you love me so!

I want you to know,
That I love you lots.
When my hair is in knots,
You gently brush to stop it hurting.
And as you are a doctor, you are always nursing,
To help me and the world.

Your hair is always curled,
But naturally blacky-brown.
And even when I am feeling down,
You cheer me up with a smile,
It cheers me up by a mile.

I want you to know,
That I love you so.

Love you, Mummy!

Ellie Pash (9)

Lime

You're a cocoon,
Soft on the inside,
Hard on the outside.
Your rays of light shine on my face,
You kick the zest into my day.
You are sour, but that's to make me better,
Without you, life would be bland.
It's nature's bell,
Just like you, a cocoon,
Waiting for a butterfly.

Nabeeha Azam

Mothers

Mothers, mothers everywhere,
Mothers are kind and will always care.
Mothers, mothers everywhere,
Whatever they look like, they're always unique.
Somehow you never need to peek,
To see if your mother's there, because she's always there in your heart.
Every day, all I really want to say is, "I love you, Mum."

Maisie-Rae Narraway

World's Best Mum

Your love has never fallen short,
You have been my only support.
To be a friend, nurse, cook and chauffeur,
Yet find time and energy as a teacher.

Sweet Mum, years have been gone long,
Since you sang a melody song.
Your sweet smile guides my way,
You're bright sunshine, lighting my day.

My mum's love and tenderness so dear,
Throughout my life you've always been near.
You are in my heart, I let you know,
I'll always be there, in good times and low.

No one can love me like you, Mum.
Happiness or sorrow, you make it fun.

Areesha Haque (12)

My Marvellous Mum

My mum is the best mum ever,
She is so kind and clever.
No one can take her from my heart,
She has been my mum from the start.

She is always there for me,
Even when I feel lonely.
I love her ever so much,
Whenever she hugs me, it's like a magical touch.

Anasha Raza

Our Mothers

Whatever we call them, they're always there,
But if they're not, then they would still care
About the things we kids do every day
And that we're on the right path all the way.

Though it won't seem fair at one's first glance,
At least let them wise ones have a chance
To remind us all of what is right
And teach us ways that we can live right.

There is (nearly) no reason why we'd want to be without
The one person who protected us all throughout
The time we spent with them in life-
Do you think you'd be successful without their support?

There are many people with jobs, like the humble reporter,
Collecting words from all, young or old
And one of them might as well be you,
You might be of that news, too.

But, just like everyone else, we start somewhere,
So that is where those people come to share
Their large wisdom, from many places.
After all, they won't just leave us helpless.

They care for us dearly, and always have,
When they laboured to keep us alive
And carried us with them all around.

We always wonder what we'd do without them,
Their overprotectiveness and their meaningful words
That has led us all to where we are now.

So this is why on this special day,
We give gratitude to our mothers today with happiness and joy
And the giving of presents which we all enjoy.
But whatever happens, they'll always be there. Love you, Mum!

Avril Megan Lansangan

My One And Only!

Dear my one and only mother,
I wouldn't want any other,
You always help me to be my best,
So on Mother's Day you deserve a rest!

You always listen to my opinions,
You are honestly worth billions,
You kiss me, hug me, make me feel loved,
And that's why to me you are beloved.

You take me places for me to have fun,
You've helped me to put my hair in a bun,
You always listen to what I want to say,
You pick me up when I feel grey.

You're so pretty inside and out,
I still love you even when you shout,
We will always be together, never apart,
Maybe not in distance but always in heart.

Emily Bryan

My mum is sweet,
Usually has a smile on her face.
Walk around and spread joy,
Yeah, that's how
I remember her.

Don't know if
She's an angel in disguise,
Or a saint, somebody holy

But what is a fact,
Is that I really do love my mum.
And that, my friends,
Will go down in history!

Chudi Patrick Onwuokwu

My Mother's Pride

Happiness has a home in her eyes,
A look of warmth that ends demise.
It sets me free,
And gives me hope.
A light in the dark,
A moon amongst the stars.
Her words speak truth,
Experience like no other
And sends me to sleep.
And I say to her,
I love you deeply.

She kept me warm during the winter,
Covering me with love.
And when I was young,
She hugged me tight,
Saying she can't wait for me to grow up.
And now I've matured,
Learnt and have been shaped.
She guided me,
And sent me on my way.
To live a life to be free,
My mother's pride is what I want to be.

Mahrou Meem

Mummies

People who sacrifice for you,
You should respect them too,
Which are mostly mummies,
That we came from their tummies.

They keep you safe,
And take you to the café,
Always keep you happy,
And change your nappy.

She always takes care,
Makes everything fair.
Has a laugh and plays with you,
She can also make you a brew.

Greatest in the world,
Makes you laugh till you hurl,
Just so funny,
They make your day so sunny.

Zohal Ahmad (10)

My Magnificent Mother

Here's to the mother who knows I'm injured
From the faint whiff of freeze spray
And the dehydrated dry debris of tears on my face
Here's to the mother who has my report card memorised
Before I even come home from school
Congratulating me on every line
Giving my confidence a boost
Here's to the mother who bends her bruised back
Looking for the monsters in my head,
And cranes her narrow neck,
(Because she never thought I'd be so much taller than her,
Even though she's a giant in kindness)
To check for the monsters in my head

Here's to the mother whose resilience has taught me to be
granite instead of steel
For steel is simply a synthetic material undergone surgery
Whereas granite has been born from the enigmatic
embrace of mother nature
Immune to the pyroclastic flows streaming down the
volcanic cheeks

Here's to the mother who I endeavour to replicate
Smiling from ear-to-ear when anyone says we look alike
Because being anything like her
Would be akin to being the second angel that fell from
Heaven
And forced Satan to stay in Hell,
So that all her children could rest in peace.

Here's to my mother
Although the six-letter word
Could never capture the trillion tonne impact she has had in my
One milligram life.

Krita Shah

The Best Mummy In The Universe

My mummy is the best,
Way better than the rest,
The best mummy in the universe.

She is warmer than her daily tea,
And does loving things for me,
The best mummy in the universe.

Her hugs are very snug,
As snug as a bug in a rug,
The best mummy in the universe.

She never fails to kiss me goodnight,
As she quietly whispers, "Sleep tight,"
The best mummy in the universe.

My mummy raised me from when I was small,
And she always catches me when I fall,
The best mummy in the universe.

She helps me feel better,
When my eyes are sad and wetter,
The best mummy in the universe.

Her cooking is incredibly yummy,
It fills everyone's tummy!
The best mummy in the universe.

She encourages me to do good on Earth,
And follow my dreams, for whatever they're worth.
The best mummy in the universe.

I will always love her and she will always love me,
After all, nobody can't love and laugh with...
The best mummy in the universe.

Holly Dimery (10)

My Mum

I have a mum,
A mum I love,
A mum who is always there for me,
A mum who loves, laughs and smiles.

I have a mum,
A mum who cares,
A mum who wants me to do well,
A mum who helps me, with everything I need.

I have a mum,
A mum who I can tell things to,
A mum who listens and understands,
A mum who gives me good advice.

I have a mum,
A mum I want to make proud,
A mum I want to please.

I have a mum I love.

Sayuri Knox (12)

Mommy

You are the most important person in the world.
You're worth more than gold.
And even if we don't always agree,
We are like a tree.

We keep the good fruit and throw the ugly ones.
My mother has the most beautiful eyes.
No one in the world is more important than you,
And for all the things you've done for me, I want to say
thank you.

Everything will happen, we will be like a screen,
Reflecting on beautiful things, as the springs.
You are my queen,
The most beautiful and good person, I have seen.

You are my point of reference, you bring me peace,
The most intelligent and most exigent.
Thou shalt always shine,
Because you are my sunshine.

First my mother, forever my friend
As in the weekend,
When we spend time together,
Between mum and daughter.

Home is where is your mother,
And I will always be there for her.
You always tell me to be positive,
You are always the person I believe,
Because without you, I could not live.

Patricia Claudia Sabau (14)

Oh Dear Mum, My Dear Mum

Oh dear Mum, my dear mum,
Every morning, you jump up with a spring.
You bang on like a drum,
But Mum, dear Mum, you just can't help but sing.
Your face is plastered on with a heavy grin,
Every morning as I rise,
However, that look would disappear fast when you had to take the bins outside.
Oh dear Mum, my dear mum.

Oh dear Mum, my dear mum,
How fast you could hustle when we were late.
Never in my life have I seen someone run so fast,
When we had to reach the green ghoulish gate.
It was as if, it was the Olympics, we went for gold and never came last.
Oh dear Mum, my dear mum,
You are superwoman in a power suit,
You strut like a star, a model in fact,
You have high aims and can shoot,

Your ideas are genius and highly stacked,
Oh dear Mum, my dear mum.

Oh dear Mum, my dear mum,
If only you truly understood,
We love you with all our hearts,
Trust me your love is just too good.
It's exquisite like a fine piece of art.

Believe when I speak though, we have nothing left to say,
We truly adore you, Mum,
Enjoy your day in the sun!

Maryam Rehan

My Mummy!

My mummy is really sweet.
I love my mummy more than the beach.
I love my mummy and she loves me,
She really is so lovely.

Together we are family,
So, I love my mum and she loves me because she is my mummy.
My mum is like 1, 2, 3 because she is always there for me!
My mummy is the best and the others can't compare.

Ellie Jim

My Mother Is The Key To Everything

My mother is the shining light in my nightmares,
She is the happiness, laughter and the beauty of me.
My mother is the harmony singing me to a peaceful sleep,
She is the sweet aroma teaching me to never give up,
My mother is a comforting blanket draped over me,
She is the key that unlocks my heart.

My mother is the crystal tears of joy encouraging me to carry on,
She is the guardian protecting me with every step of my life,
My mother is the lullaby rocking me to sleep,
She is the last piece of the puzzle,
My mother is the rainbow of all my emotions.
She is the key that unlocks my smile.

My mother is the hope guiding me to paradise,
She is the angel telling me to do the right things,
My mother is the one who is always there for me,
She is the wishes that have come true,
My mother is everything to me,
She is the key that will unlock my future.

Lamisa Akram

The World's Best Mum

The world's best mum,
Is so fun,
I'm the lucky one,
As it's my mum!

Mum likes playing with me,
Much more than watching TV,
I'm having so much fun,
With my lovely mum!

For me my mum will always be there,
Her love, no one else can compare,
My mum is simply divine,
And you won't find a mum like mine!!!

Namratha Devendra

Our Mum Is The Best

Our mum is the best because she is loving and caring,
Our mum is the best because she is always there for us,
Our mum is the best because she always spends time with us,
She is the best mum ever!

Jamie Leigh & Lacey Sophia King

Thank You For Being The Best Mum

Thank you for doing so many things for me since I was little.
Thank you for explaining things I don't know the meaning of.
Thank you for being funny and making me laugh.
Thank you for doing so many things to make my life easier.

Thank you for making my juice every day.
Thank you for organizing my weekends for me.
Thank you for letting me go to the shop every Friday.
Thank you for being understanding when I say mean things I don't mean.
Thank you for trying to understand my feelings.

Thank you for being the best mum!

Leah Kelly (15)

Roses are red,
Violets are blue,
Mum, you're my sunshine,
In all the things you do.

My mum is special,
Above all the rest,
She is the nicest person I've ever met.

My mum is extraordinary, she plays her part.
She will always be a handprint on my heart.

Dear Mum, you're considerate and true,
When I grow up, I want to be just like you.
As I close off my poem, I would like to say thank you in
every way.

Kamsiyochi Ukonu (10)

What Does Your Mum Do For You?

What does your mum do for you?
It's a number let me guess, 4, 5, 8, 10,
Well, my mum does a lot more than that!

She takes me to different countries like,
Malaysia and Sri Lanka,
She teaches me loads of new things,
She's kind and caring,
Not just to me, to others too,
You wouldn't be born without your mother!

Your mother is kind, caring, brave, beautiful,
Helpful, loving, amazing, peaceful, divine and adorable,
Now don't think there aren't any more

But... don't you get your hopes up
My mum's the best mum!

Amritaa Devendra

World's Best Mum

W ow, our mum is amazing!
O h yes - three boys she is raising
R unning around doing this and that
L ots of sorting out when I'm a brat
D oesn't like it when we fight or moan
S ometimes she will have a groan

B est buddies and companions we are
E veryone loves a ride in her car
S uper mum to Ethan, Thomas and me
T he world's best mum to us three

M ummy, Mummy, Mummy
U nderneath you are so funny
M ummy, Mummy, Mummy

Jacob Saum

The Wonders Of A Mum

Teddy bear hugs and lots of kisses,
Are the things mums love to do.
While she zooms through the house,
Searching for something else to do.

Oh, my mum is like a lovely rose,
That is blooming beautifully in the sun.
If I am bored, we will always have fun,
She's always there for me, she never goes.

She's the no.1 mum,
I very much agree.
She will always have a cup of tea.

Gladly I'll give my heart out to you,
Some yummy chocolates and flowers too.
You're more wonderful than a shooting star,
What a wonderful mum you truly are.

Irza Tariq

Who My Mother Is...

The biggest present life has to offer is her,
Which no one can destroy.
Even in the darkest places, she glows,
Like an unstoppable light bulb, that has endless love for
me.
She is unselfish and caring, a deep devotion, a miracle from
Heaven.

I always have a shoulder to cry on and a person to look up
to,
She is caring and protective.
Her soul is always with me.
Her praising words get me through my struggles.
She is the sunlight in my day.

Her heart made from the purest of gold.
My best friend, all I am is because of her.
She has given me the gift to live
And taught me how to use it.

She's taught me right from wrong,
Good to bad, and I want to let her know.

Avni Avni

Happy Mother's Day

Mum, you are so brill it's really hard to say,
How grateful I am to you,
For being my mum your way.

Now let's give a cheer for Mum!
In our house, her voice is law.
I put her above all else
Except my PS4.

Rohan Steels Polhill

My Mum

My mum is my sun,
She brings light to my dark,
She brings all the fun,
Making my life a roller coaster park.

I love my roller coaster,
But it seems to go so fast.
My only wish is that my roller coaster lasts.

Keira Sheldon

My Mum

My mum is caring, kind and compassionate.
My mum does cooking, cleaning and washing.
My mum is the greatest, bestest mum ever!

Clodagh Sheldon

Remembering Mothers

Remembering mothers
Think big, think wild
Think that you own this world in style
Think out of the box to say yes to your demands

Power is key, power is famous
Powers for mothers in our commands and dimensions
Speak near, speak far
Our mothers are here to speak for justice and peace

Strong and courageous, brave and curious, act like mother
nature
Hear us today as we follow your footsteps to your way

Mothers, mothers
When the time comes
The reward of gratitude
Reflects your personalities
As you have had too much
On your shoulders
With worry and pain
Your ability to summon light
Has let out a collective groan
Which always saves the day.

Chidera Ugoagbala

My Mummy

M y mum is the best mum in the world,
Y ears went by with my mummy Ada.

M y mum taught me lots of things,
U nicorns are her favourite animal.
M y mummy loves me, just as I love her.
M agical, beautiful, amazing, caring and loving are the perfect words to describe my mum.
Y es! Yes! I am SO happy and lucky this is my mum. No one has a better mum than me.

Flavia Spence

 For You...

For you...
I would pick the finest fruit all the way from Kent.
For you...
I would book you the luxury holiday you always wanted.
For you...
I would do all the washing and cleaning so you can put your feet up.
For you...
I would get you the watch of your dreams from Michael Kors.
For you...
I would do anything to see you smile!

Afia Adu-Gyamfi

Dear Mom

There is no other love,
It fits around your heart,
Like a hand in a glove,
Can't be cracked with a dart.

It was there when you were small,
And still no end in sight.
From the time you were tall,
It still hasn't taken flight.

Bigger than a spark,
Gives you the light,
To never enter the dark,
All remains bright.

For me this is the start,
A glove that won't fray,
Wrapped around your heart,
Happy Mother's Day.

Malaika Farhan Ashraf

My Amazing Mum

The one that loves me,
The one that laughs, sometimes at me,
The one who always shares my tears,
The one who lifts me up, when I feel down.
This is the perfect mum for me.

She may no longer have to feed me,
Or get me dressed every day,
But I will never lose a place within her heart.
We may not always get along, but I love her,
And she loves me!
She is my mum, unlike any other,
The most unique.
This is why she is so amazing. I love you, Mum.

Paige Brigid Jones

My Marvellous Mother

She has eyes that sparkle like stars,
And a smile that reaches Mars,
She is spectacular at cooking,
You don't need a booking,

She has a heart filled with magic and love,
She is as glorious as a dove,
When I am scared she gives me a hug,
She is sensible and doesn't hurt creatures like a ladybug,

This is why I use this special day to celebrate her,
She is my marvellous mother!

Sukhman Kaur

Everybody Says...

Everybody says their mum is the best,
But mine truly is, there is no contest.
She is the queen of cooking, the queen of good looking,
She's the queen of my house.

Everybody says their mum is an inspiration,
But mine should be known for that across the nation.
My mum is the rarest of the rare,
Because she shows me love, attention and care!

I wrote this poem to wish my mum, grandma and nan a
happy Mother's Day. I wouldn't wish for my mum to be
different in any way.

I love my mum!

Jojo Moloney

Pain

The first time I meet with someone,
When they have a prick,
They start to cry,
I am hated.

Then, when plucking a gnasher,
The child starts to cry,
I am hated.

Then, a dad who's broken his arm,
I am hated,
Once again.

A mum who's about to hear a patter of tiny feet,
Hugs me tightly,
With shock I say,
"Until now no one has liked me."

Going past,
A mum feeding,
He bites her,
I say, "I'll go away,
I don't want to hurt you."

The mum replies stroking the baby,
"There is no need to go away,
This is all part of being a mum."

"Only a mum likes me,
No one else in the world likes me."

Mum replies,
"Hug me tightly; yes, I love you,
Without pain,
There won't be any mums."

Today is your day, Mum,
So happy Mother's Day.

Rishika Raghunandanan

Believe

Nanna,
You brighten up my day,
Even if you're far away,
In hospital or home,
You will never be alone,
As I am always thinking of you.
Wherever you may be,
You have my admiration,
And brighten up the nation.
You've taught me right from wrong,
You are so strong.
The days are long without you,
So much I need to tell you.
So many places to visit,
And many sights to see,
Together we will conquer this,
Just you wait and see!

Natalie Elizabeth Ruddle

Made By Mum

My mother's food
Is delicious.
Not due to the spices
Or the ingredients.

It boils over
The heat of pure love
And a dash of laughter
Is added in.

There is a slight hint
Of disagreements but
That's what balances it out,
And makes the flavour special.

There are stories
And arguments,
Hugs,
Everything a mother does is included.

And it is served with
A side of kisses
And a warm
Loving smile.

Mawadda Edbagi

A Mother's Love

A mother's love in the air,
This connection will never tear
You gave birth to me,
And it would be a she
You love me so much,
I would never die from your touch
We can never be apart,
I would receive love from your heart
Your heart is worth more than wealth,
With your help I am now twelve
For Mother's Day,
Your old memories when you play
You are so caring,
I gave you that gold necklace you are wearing
The love that you show,
Makes me want to know
How you became this beautiful lady,
However, you are never so shady
To our own ability,
You work with agility
Your love is so pure,
You fix us with a cure
I love you, Mum,
I will stay in your life till the last crumb.

Anika Anpalagan

World Optimum Mother

For the endearment you give,
The sagacity you share,
All the ways you bless my life
With your delicate heart.
I love you as my mom, the wonderful woman,
Who has done more for me than any other person in this world.
On this special day, I want to say thank you for all the love you gave me.
I want to say thanks for raising me as a superior child.

Joyra Subur

World's Best Mum

What is a mother?
Someone who cares for their babies.
But doesn't care for another,
They make their mums have grandbabies.

My point of view is different,
My mum cares for others,
Her slangs are current,
Unlike most mothers.

This day is really special,
Because we are celebrating mums all over the world.
You have to be as sharp as a pencil,
So we can make mum's day like a dream world.

This message I am about to tell,
Is for all you children out there.
Let it ring like a bell,
And not into the air.

Look after your mum while you are young,
So you won't regret it later in life,
Also, if it is at the tip of your tongue,
Say it out before it gets cut with a knife.

Chisom Ubochi

The World's Best Mum

You have always been there for me,
In times of great happiness and in times of deep grief.
Every step I take in life, you are there for me, holding my
hand.

In my depths of sorrow, you sit with me,
You always cheer me up and make me chuckle.
You rescue me from my sadness,
Will someone tell me, are all mums like this?

When it comes to learning,
You're always eager to help me, because you want me to
be the best.
When I win an award, all your joyful tears can make a scarf
wet.
Me, you and my sister are always enjoying ourselves
together.
We've made so many magnificent memories together.

You're super mummy because you always stay by my side.
You are my fairy godmother because you grant all my
wishes and take absolute care of me.
You've written my past and now we continue to write my
future.

You're the world's best mum,
And that's why I love you so much.
You're so kind, amazing, affectionate and big-hearted.
I love you, Mum, you're the world's best mum.

Parisha Jobanputra (12)

My Marvellous Mum

My mum is great, she is the best.
She helps me practise for every spelling test.
She gives me clothes, she gets me toys.
We bake together which she really enjoys.

She lets me go to different clubs,
Including drama and cubs.
When I have been really good all week,
She gives me pocket money, now that's sweet.

On each birthday she gives me,
Super cool presents, way more than three.
I love her more than cherry pie.
She's cooler than the breeze up high.
So thank you, Mum, for being so fun!

Ruby Holbrook

My mum smells of flowers, buttercups and cake,
If you ever see her, you will realise how much happiness she
can make.

She gives me the biggest bear-hugs that you will ever see,
Next time she may squeeze the life out of me.

She bakes the best sweets in the world,
But be careful because your stomach might explode.

My mum is terrific, amazing and wonderful.
She is the best.

Lucia Kyoko Rapisarda Okamoto

World's Best Mum

She,
Yes she,
Who has supported me through everything,
Is no other than my mum.

She,
Yes she,
Who is beautiful,
Is no other than my mum.

She,
Yes she,
Who has thrown sweet tantrums on me,
Is no other than my mum.

She,
Yes she,
Who has given birth to me,
Is no other than my mum.

Sweet,
Sweet,
I find a shower of sweets in you,
The kitchen comes alive because of you!

She,
Yes she,
The person I dedicated this poem to,
Is no other than my mum.

How do I thank you?

Jil Shah (8)

My Amazing Mummy!

Thank you for being my mum,
My guardian,
My boss,
My housekeeper,
My laundrette,
My nurse,
My chef,
My driver,
My personal assistant,
My cheerleader.
You are all of that and more,
My teacher,
My protector,
My confidant,
My friend.
My own special mummy xx

Lilian Agombar

What Do I Love About My Mummy?

What do I love about my mummy?
It is not how she looks, or how she is funny.
It's not what she'd wear,
Or how she'd do her hair.
It's the love she gives to me,
And knowing that it will always be.
Whether I am right or wrong,
She'll be by my side, and always strong.
She works so hard all of the day,
But will always make time with me to play.
She will always be my best friend,
And whatever the problem, she will mend.
Every night she makes me dinner,
Making sure I don't go any thinner.
Any time I am feeling down,
I know that she will always be around.
I love her so, and always will,
Whenever she appears, I get a thrill.
And that is why I love my mummy,
It is not how she looks, or how she is funny.

Ellie-May Worrall

Oh Great Mummy

To you, oh great Mummy,
A little present from someone,
That was once in your tummy,
Is it a book, plane or something fun?
It might be all of these, oh great Mum,
Now fun I hear you say,
From your little son,
It's Mother's Day!
To oh great Mummy, have a fantastic Mother's Day,
With lots of treats and lots of fun,
From your little youngster,
From your tum.

Alexander Wang Mirza

Mums

Mothers are great,
They never make you go to school late.

When you are feeling sleepy,
Or have been weepy,
Mummies are always there,
To show love and care.

Mummies are funny,
They bore you from their tummy.

Mums are clever,
Before you go to school,
They tell you the weather.

Mums are nice,
They buy you things at any price.

So whatever you call 'em
Mum, Mother, Mummy.
They're always there,
And show tender care.

Chidera Opara (8)

My Mum Is Not A Witch

My mummy's not a witch,
And this is how I know.
No spiky claws of hers I've seen,
No stretchy gloves, not red, not green.

My mummy's not a witch,
And this is how I know.
She's got bubbly, see-through spit,
But witches... oh it's blue.
She sticks to me like glue,
And my brother too.

My mummy's not a witch,
And this is how I know.
She doesn't have a bald head,
And never forgets to make my bed.

My mummy's not a witch,
And this is how I know.
Her feet are not square,
And I tickle her toes.
I like to follow her,
Wherever she goes!

Noah Elliott (6)

I Love My Mum

My mum's hugs are as warm as hot chocolate on a cold day.
Her smile is as bright as the sun.
Her cooking is as yummy as feasting with royalty.
My mum's favourite colour is purple, like the colour of the sunset.
Her favourite animal is an elephant because like her they have a great memory.
She likes cups of tea, like a hug in a mug.
I love my mum, like she loves me!

Oscar Smallpiece

A Mother's Colours Of The Rainbow

Red is your fire when you fight through pain, your inspiring endurance as you break every chain.

Orange is your leniency when you're firm, but fair, your controlled discipline that shows that you care.

Yellow is your happiness when you laugh and smile, a jocund sight I see that makes every day worthwhile.

Green is your nature of bringing forth life. I love the brothers you gave me (despite the strife).

Blue is your consolation when I am heartbroken, how I find strength in the words you've spoken.

Indigo is your ability to save and invest. My brothers do it too, as they've learnt from the best.

Violet is your smarts and your ever-increasing success. I have to say, Mother, I am quite impressed.

It makes sense to say you're most like the colour white, a symbol of Heaven, purity and light.

White is more than just one colour, although it doesn't seem so. Like you, white is every colour of the heavenly rainbow.

Deborah Oluwateniola Olorunfemi

My Mum

My mum, she runs and runs,
You can't overtake her.
She is faster than ever,
When my mum does a marathon, she is the best!

I love to do it too,
My mum is amazing,
She can beat a racecar.
If you don't believe me, go to the next marathon.

Lily Jones

Mum

Mum,
You've always been there for me,
Through thick and thin.
I'm sorry I wasn't more open,
I never let you in.

I'm trying to make things better,
Though I can hardly say I'm winning.
And yet you're always there,
You have been since the beginning.

You put up with my anger,
My swiftly changing moods.
With all my fussy eating,
And unhealthy foods.

You've never not believed in me,
Encouraging me always.
Never giving up on me,
Even on bad days.

I'm glad you're my mum,
I appreciate all you do.
We all love you, Mama,
And we know you love us too.

Abi Green

The World's Best Mum Belongs To Me

Your tender smile guides my way,
You're the sunshine that lights up my day.

You tell me what's right and what's wrong,
I pray to God you stay for long.

You're a caring doctor that knows how I feel,
Your hugs and kisses do really heal.

I'm as happy as can be,
The world's best mum belongs to me!

Happy Mother's Day!

Mariam Kaid

Mother Like No Other

I love my mother,
She's like no other.
She's my best friend.
It will never end.
She feeds me.
Sometimes we go to the sea.
I love her food.
It puts me in a good mood.

Cormaic McElhatton

Happy Mother's Day

Your love.
Your heart.
Has never fallen apart.

Even when you're faced with darkness.
Up and down life goes.
You go with the blows.

To the best mum in the world.
So don't leave me.
And let us just be.

You are the best.
You are always close to my chest.
Happy Mother's Day.

Lara Valadas

World's Best Mum

You're the best mum
Mum, you're as beautiful as a queen
Mum, you're as wonderful as an elephant
Mum, you're as skilful as a grizzly bear
Mum, you're as strong as a lion
Mum, you're as flexible as a fish
Mum, you're magnificent like Jesus
Mum, you're as joyful as a newborn baby
Mum, you're as truthful as God
Mum, you're as amazing as a new species
Mum, you're as cool as Will.i.am
Mum, you're everything to me
Mum, you're as peaceful as a butterfly
Mum, you're as musical as a lullaby
Mum, you're as important as being healthy
And now I've got to say I love you like everything
And happy Mother's Day!

Munachi Ubochi

Best Mom

M ommy, Mommy, you're the best, you are better than all the rest.

O n Mother's Day we celebrate you, to show you that my love is true

M ommy, you are kind, you look after me and make me so happy - don't you see

M ommy, you have a great big heart, I hate it when we are apart

Y ou're the best mom ever.

Rosie Allen-Richards

Mommy & Me

What a great way to start our life in Mummy's tummy,
All the kicks and bouncing I did to her,
Neither did she complain nor she bothered.
Yummy food coming down to me in the womb,
Yum! Yum! They were tasty and healthy too.
Slowly, I was growing big and big.
And she was happy seeing me in her scans.
One fine day I saw the world through her.
Crying! Crying but she always comforted and calmed me down,
Rock-a-bye Baby! Made me fall asleep soon!
Cosy in her gentle arms was so relaxing.
Crawling and walking, holding her hands was a blessing,
Me and my mom were busy walking and talking.
Mischievous was I with my dad, but they never get mad.
Time flew and then came my little sissy,
And we both always love to hug and kiss.
Mom is busy cleaning and cooking,
But to get in her 'Kitchen Restaurant' there's no booking.
Guiding and advising all through my life,
Love to cuddle you like my teddy, wrapped in a duvet on your beddy.
We love each other in our family,
And would like to finish saying, Father and Mother, I love you!

Sakshi Suji (6)

The Most Special Jewel Of Them All

If I could give you a diamond,
for every lesson, because of you, I learned.
If I could give you a ruby,
for every time you made me feel happy.
If I could give you a sapphire,
for all the times you lifted me higher.
If I could give you an opal,
for whenever you've made me feel special.
Then you'd have enough riches,
that they would almost reach the skies.
But even the sparkle in these gems,
could not compare to the sparkle in your eyes.
But I have no diamonds, no opals, no jewels,
as I am sure you're well aware.
But not even that gift would amount to,
your trust, your love and your care.
A jewel is precious, beautiful and treasured,
a mother is all of those things too.
Because a mother is the most special jewel of them all,
so, Mum, I want you to know I love you.

Mirha Butt

My Mum Is The Best

All mums are excellent but mine is extra sweet
Her heart is so big we hear it beat
Her love for me grows and grows
I even love the way she ties my hair in a bow
My mum is the best, she should be the queen
She is as clever as a bean
When it's night she shares us some treats
Putting us to bed is a real mean feat
Mother's Day will be a lovely day
We'll have so much fun, we'll play
Over again I will say
My mum is the best.

Ava Becker

My Mum

My mum does so much for me,
She picks me up when I am down,
Destroys my fears,
Turns my frown upside down,
Dries my tears.

She cooks,
She cleans,
My hair, she preens.
Soon she will have to deal with a teen.
Hopefully I don't annoy her with every fibre of my being.

She's not only my mum, definitely not,
My mum is my best friend too.
I hope you think with nostalgia,
What does your mum mean to you?

Chiamaka Tamzin Waudby

The World's Greatest Mum

Our mothers are so helpful,
They cook for us, something special.
When times are down, they help us rise.
Up and up, beyond the blue skies.

We never really realise how special mothers are,
And sometimes in arguments we seem to fall apart.
But our mums are so great to us,
That's why we give them all of our love,
To mums out there.
Thank you for everything, Mum!

Kayin Duran Pereira

Mums Are Amazing

Mums are great
Mums are cool
They cook, clean and do fun stuff
Mums are pretty
They play with us
Do homework with us
Mums are awesome
We love our mum very much
Mums love us forever.

Amy Dryburgh

My Mother

M y mummy is great
Y ou are the greatest mum in the world

M um, you are amazing
O ut of all the mums in the world, you're the best
T he most unique in the universe
H appiness is being with you
E xtremely educated, epic and totally exclusive
R eally special, smart and so amazing.

Sophie Denise Wilkinson

My Mum Smells Of Fruity Perfume

My mum smells like lovely fruity perfume.
My mum looks pretty and so joyful and kind.
I hear my mummy reading me bedtime stories as my eyes drift down.
She does really yummy cooking - Sunday roasts, creamy curry and gooey cake.
If I didn't have my mum I would feel so sad and empty.
Oh, I love my mum so much.

Betsy Kirk

Mum, you are amazing
I love the way you sing
You are a bell that goes *bing!*
Every night you wish me sweets dreams
It seems
Like you're the sun and I'm the planets circling you.
Today is your day, Mum
Not the day you sum,
Happy Mother's Day, Mum.

Lena Hanna Thlon

Mother's Day

My mum is the best
So today's the day to take a rest,
Here are some flowers
And some chocolates too.
I'll give her a kiss,
That's one thing I can do.
She might want a Rolo
Or a minty Polo.
I would do her hair
Very beautifully nice.
We will play lots of games
About our pretty names.

I'll make her bed
And stroke her head.
We will have a nice lunch,
A whole big bunch.
We have some fun,
Some fun outside.
The day is about to end
So I must say goodnight
She will always be my mum,
My pretty mum.

Olivia McColl

Amazing Mum!

My mum is really the best
And trust me, she never rests.
She is a pro cook,
Just take a look.

She wakes up in the morning
When everybody is snoring.
She is like a fairy
And never gets weary.

My mum makes sure the house is clean
And I love when everything gleams.
Her energy is everlasting power
It increases every hour.

My packed lunch tastes great,
So many flavours to learn and create.
She always bakes
Delicious cakes.

I can tell everybody on a beating drum
I love you, Mum!

Aaria Sardar

Mum

My mum, my mum, she's as sweet as a plum
And as beautiful as a bouquet of roses,
And an egg that never perishes.
Neither does her love for me.

Her voice is as dazzling and exquisite as an orchestra,
Larks and hummingbirds are even jealous.
Her beaming eyes are even visible to the night sky.
She's as busy as a bee,
Taking care of me.

Jessica Lezama

World's Best Mum

My mum is caring
My mum is sharing
My mum is powerful too
My mum is cheerful
My mum is fun
She fills the day with glory like the morning sun
She treasures me with a heart full of love
Every day I remember loving you
My mum.

Parneet Shanan

My Mother

M y mother is the best
O f the best
T he most helpful and
H appy mom
E verything that she does for me is just
R ight.

Noah Sayed (10)

My Mom

My mommy is funny
She tucks me into bed
This is why I love her
And I will never be parted from my mom.

Rose Sayed (9)

My Dear Mommy

I love you, Mommy
My dear mommy
You make me happy when I am sad
I want to tell you that I love you
When I am with you I am so glad.

Ella Sayed (5)

I Love You, Mummy

I love you, Mummy, you are so funny and you make me smile
We laugh and play every day and I love being your child
You make me happy all the time
You read me books that are really funny and they rhyme
And they make me sleepy just before bedtime
I love you, Mum, you're so nice, you're so nice and kind
I love you, Mummy, you are one of a kind.

Lewis Lachlan Cameron

Mothers

What a blessing a mother can be,
A gift of love for eternity.
Nurturing you from the very start,
With the beating of a heart.
You're so many things to so many people,
And today you're celebrated for the beautiful person you
are.
When I think of those,
I know and love,
I can't think of one
You don't tower above.
You are the better by far,
More than all the rest.
These four words say it all:
"Mom, you're the best."
However,
Mothers hold their children's hands for a short while,
But their hearts forever.
I know that no matter what
Your spirit will be with me always.
When I see a bird chirping on a nearby branch
I will know it is you singing to me.
You will always be with me.

Caitlin Emma-Jo Francis

Letter To My Mum

Dear Mum,
You are there when days are glum.
I love you,
And I know you feel the same too.

You are there in my dreams,
No matter how weird they seem.
You are the hero protecting me from slaughter,
On this special day, from your daughter.

Amazing-Grace Oluwadara Ojo

Mums Are...

Mums are wonderful
Mums are beautiful
Mums are adventurous
Mums are generous
Mums are loving
Mums are caring
Mums are my everything
But there's one thing
They love you
With your angel wings.

Tamara Krawiec (10)

Mummy's The Best

Big brown eyes
A lovely smile
She puts me to bed
And doesn't make a mess
I love her so
She is the best mum in the universe
She is the number one mum in the world
Mummies are really helpful
They are honest and kind
They're the best thing in the world that has ever happened
to us.

Ameya Parvati Polavajram

My Mother's My Angel

My mother's my angel,
She's always been there
She may not be a saint
But she's always cared.

My mother's my angel,
She's always been there
She has the greatest smile
Nothing could compare.

My mother's my angel,
She's always been there
She may not have been the richest
But her love was always there.

My mother's my angel,
She's always been there
She is so beautiful
It could make the other mothers feel despair.

My mother's my angel,
She's always been there
Even when I was losing my marbles
And no one else cared.

Trey Devonte McLean

My Mum

My mum is the world's best
But what distinguishes her from all the rest?
Her caring, comforting, loving touch,
Her big, warm, friendly hug,
She helps me out whenever I need,
It seems she has done not a single bad deed,
My mum loves to see others happy,
But sometimes she can get a bit sappy,
My mum is the world's best,
And these things are what distinguishes her from all the rest.

Katie Susan Walker

World's Best Mum

Have you ever wondered who has the world's best mum?
Well it's a very simple sum
As my mum is not like some.

Her imaginative mind can come up with all sorts,
And of course she's a master at sports,
Even though she takes care of four kids,
She will still have enough time to cook ribs!

She knows me like the back of her hand,
And can name any brand,
My mum loves to cook
But not just by the book.

Her golden-brown hair flows in the light of day,
When she's around there's never a cloud of grey,
Her stunning brown eyes shine when the bright sun shows,
She can pull off billions of different coloured bows.

My mum is the world's best
It's impossible to compare her to the rest.

Heba Qaisar Mirzazada

Mother's Day Poem For My Mum

M arvellous mums are happy on Mother's Day.

O ther mums are special to their kids but mine is more special to me.

T here are special mums in the world but my mum is more special.

H ere in the world, mums are helpful.

E aster eggs make mums happy.

R ed rose for my mum.

S inging makes my mum happy.

D inner for my mum because she rocks

A nd she is special.

Y ay! It's Mother's Day.

Victor Akintula

I Love My Mum

I love my mum,
She's kind and sweet,
She's there for me day and night,
No matter what.

My mum is the best,
She's full of love,
She cares for us every day,
And always keeps us safe.

No one is nicer than my mum,
She's always helpful,
And full of fun,
She never relaxes because of us.

No one can compare to my mum,
Even if they try,
It's just too hard,
That's how good she really is.

Mother's Day is when we show our love,
To our mums,
Who need a break,
Like my mum.

Mother's Day is special to my mum,
She runs around after us every day,
Making her exhausted,
That's the day we need to give her a rest and show our
love.

Every day my mum will share her love,
And show us that she cares,
Even if she's tired from the day before,
It doesn't change her attitude.

You couldn't get a mum better than mine,
Even if you tried.

Imogen Eve Seddon

My Mum

I was down and desperate
Hopeless and afraid
I thought I was alone
With no one at my aid

But she proved me wrong
As she always will
No matter what I've done
She will be with me still

She lifted me up
Put me on my feet
Dusted me off gently
And these words did she speak

When I brought you in this world
Love was in my heart
You are my treasure, my one true love
I never want to part

If you ever need me
I'll always be here
I'll shelter you from the rain
Whatever you're going through
I'm here to share your pain

My mum is so supportive
She's always ready to share
So I really want to thank her
For always being there.

Amy Saunders

Mother's Day

M y mum is the best
O ut of all the others
T he most awesome mum is mine
H appiness is what she brings every day
E ach mum is unique but mine is the most amazing
R esting on the sofa for her is very rare because
S he is busy making my day

D ay by day she helps me
A nd makes me laugh, it's
Y our chance to celebrate such an amazing mum.

Wiktoria Chodakowska

Mother, What Would I Do Without You?

Mother, what would I do without you?
You are like my missing shoe,
You mean the world to me,
So let this love be.

You brighten up every day,
You brighten up my heart,
You play a big part in my life.
What would I do without you?

You are my treasure,
You are the best mother.
It is such a pleasure...
What would I do without you?

Even though I am bad,
You always don't get mad,
Instead you make me glad.
What would I do without you?
###
You share your love with me,
And I can easily see.
You are my universe...
What would I do without you?

You taught me how to live,
You taught me how to give,
You taught me everything.
What would I do without you?

You are my missing piece to a jigsaw.
You are my missing piece to life.
You are my missing piece to the future.
What would I do without you?
What would I do without you?

Mother, what would I do without you?

Abishan Jesuthas

The World's Best Mum

Mum, I really love you,
You always help me with everything I do,
Mum, you support me with love, and you are special,
Your hugs make me feel warm and protected,
You are a huge part of my life
Because you were there since and before I was born,
To finish telling you that you are the best mum and I'm proud of you,
I just wanted to tell a little bird to deliver this message to you...
I love you just as you are!

Olivia Peddle

My Inspiration

The never-ending hugs and kisses
Never leaving or abandoning
Always there, never gone
Always giving praise
Helps you when you make mistakes
Who am I talking about?
Your mum
Your kind and amazing mum.
I love you so much, Mum.

Ella Luisa MacCulloch

About My Mum

My mum is special, fabulous
My mum is kind, helpful and always marvellous
She's recommended as my hero
My mum is the number one mum in the whole entire world
My mum is the best mum
My mum is powerful, strong
My mum never gives up
She just keeps going
Until everything is just right.

Freya Turner

My Mother

My mother is kind and dear
And with her I have nothing to fear
I love my mom so
From head to toe
My mother would win any prize
In my eyes
From nose to toes
She's as pretty as a rose
I love Mom past Mars
To the stars and beyond
As sure as the breeze

Through the trees
And the tumbling stream round the rocks
These sounds to me
Mean my mom loves me lots.

Savannah Le Roux

Mother's Day

What should I get Mum for Mother's Day?
Breakfast in bed on a silver tray?
Or a pretty pink purse, or a flower bouquet?
What should I get Mum for Mother's Day?

Some shoes! But sis' got some for her last year,
Some earmuffs... but that makes it hard to hear,
A trip to the pub, but Mum doesn't like beer,
Or a dream catcher, so at night she'll have nothing to fear?

But what my mum would love the most,
Is not a jumper or a Sunday roast,
Or a trip to the zoo, or a trip to the coast.
It's not a bike, or a 'Best Mum' mug,
It's none of those... it's just a loving hug!

Sophie Benham

Mum's Simply The Best

My mum,
Doesn't make a crumb.
Ask her for fancy dress,
What will it be?
It'll be nice.
What about Ginger Spice?

Oh my mum is simply the best,
So from all that hard work,
You must take a rest,
You'll take me to school,
Maybe after, a swimming pool!
You'll be the best mum in my life,
Whilst being David's wife.

So please, Mum,
Accept this as a gift,
And put it on,
Your Christmas list!

Lucy Anne Rose

My Mum

My poem is short and sweet
About my mum who I would like to treat
My mum is the best
She by far beats all the rest
Although she sometimes shouts at me
I know she loves me as much as can be.

Ethan Reilly

This Is How Much I Love You

You are the final piece to my puzzle
Without you I would always struggle
To be the best I can be
Together you and I make we.

I miss you the second you are gone
And then when I see you at dawn
Life suddenly doesn't seem such a yawn
Because I love you and you keep me strong.

To the best mummy who will ever live
For all the things you give
Like kisses and cuddles
Happy Mother's Day with all my love, no trouble.

Charlie Miller

All Of My Female Figures

I look at my mother every day
And wonder whether she moulded her life with clay.
We have always been close,
She is like a big rose.
I admire everything she does and has done,
Especially getting me those cherry buns.
All I want to say
Is a big thank you for making my day
I love you!

However old she is,
I always give her a kiss.
My grandmother can be crazy
And a little bit lazy.
I love her dearly,
Even in her bright orange jumper standing clearly.
She is my beloved role model
And my saviour gospel.
I love you!

I don't always see her that often,
But every time I do she gives me tons of presents,
Even if she doesn't have enough cents.
She's never cruel to me,
Instead she gives me warm tea.
My aunt is also my female figure.

She might be younger,
But she's a stunner.
I love her more than ever,

Even though she's not that clever.
My sister is my biggest supporter, and my female figure.

Selina Okonkwo

World's Best Mum

My mum is the best
Because she gives me toys.
Mum, thank you

For all the hugs and kisses.
My mum is the best
Because she treats me with sweets.
Mum, thank you
For letting me feed the meerkats.
My mum is the best
Because she loves me!

Isabelle Paige Rowland

The Best Mum Ever

When you see her eyes glittering in the sun,
You know when she's around it's going to be fun.
When you hear her soothing voice,
You think of an angel, it's like you have no choice.
When you are sad or scared,
After her hugs you will no longer feel mad.
She is as pretty as a flower,
And when you see her smile you know she has superpowers.
They come in all shapes and forms,
But no matter what, she's my amazing mum and I couldn't
be more sure.
And the best part of the day is when we all say
Happy Mother's Day!

Chloe Yuille

Mummy

Hugs and kisses
A friendly face
A light in the darkness
When you need it most
She takes care of all your problems
That you can't fix yourself
So thank you, Mummy
For being there when I need you most
With your experience and knowhow.

Alice Rose Wintle

My Magic Mum

My mum is magic, did you know?
She can swim with dolphins
And she can go underwater,
In the desert and
All around the world.

My mum is magic, can't you see?
She can sing the sweetest song,
Just for me!

Together we learn science,
Fun as fun can be!
She helps me with my spelling
And is as busy as a bee!

My mum is magic.
She can fly in the air.
She can swing with monkeys
And go everywhere.

I love my magic mum
And she loves me!
I will never let go of her,
And neither will she,
Let go of me!

Paige Vernon

A Mum Is The One Who

A mum is the one who loved you first,
Loving you even before giving birth,
Has all the time in the world
Yet cherishes every second.

A mum is the one who has your back,
The one who is willing to cut you some slack,
A bond so strong,
Will always last so long.

A mum is the one who knows what to do,
She is also the one who can see right through,
You may not always see eye to eye,
But you know she will always be by your side.

Ellie Bevan

Mummy, Mummy, I love you
Above the sky
There is no one just like you
Mummy, Mummy, I love you
So here's a poem to celebrate you
And on this happy day
I am glad to have you.

Olivia Paren

My Mother Stands For

Many wonderful things you did for me
You are the Only mum I love
The Times we spent together watching films
A heart of Happiness that's full of memories,
An Extraordinary mother,
A Reliable person who I can always count on.

Mayriam Adagbon

Mum's Poem

When it's dark and I'm scared
You turn the lights on and you are there
To hold my hand and comfort me
You tell me I'm brilliant and funny
When kids grow they call you 'Mum'
But to me you'll always be Mummy and truckloads of fun
You work very hard to pay for the bills
But when we are together we are always chilled
You give me clothes and a roof over my head
And tuck me in before I go to bed
Let me play outside and in
To play football and Fortnite to go for the win
Make me put my leftovers in the bin
For twelve years an eternity for
You look at my bedroom and see the messy floor
Then we pull our sleeves up and finish that chore
You save lives every day
Especially mine because you make sure I'm never late
You work hard for the NHS
But to me you're mine and the very best
You bought me an Xbox and a phone
When I get bored or when I'm alone
You clap when I sing to the Greatest Show
When I'm angry, when I'm sad
You rub my back and hold my hand
To tell me it's okay
To tell me that you feel different every day
To you, you legend,
Your name is Mum
You are the best
Even though you have a smelly bum.

William Oldland

My Mom

My mom is a bouquet of flowers that never rots
As beautiful as a rose
When you look at her you'll see her beauty
Her eyes are as exquisite as the beaming sun
She's the love that came into my life
Even if I was rich, without her I'd be lost.

Vanessa Lezama

I Love My Mum

I love my mum
She is fun
She's like a friend
But she's with me till the end
She always supports me
And never bores me
And when I'm heartbroken
She's constantly there to tell me
No matter what everything will be alright
That's when I got a fright
And from then she never left my sight
You are my sunlight, Mum
Guiding me away from the dark shadows
She always calls me dear
Throughout my life I know you're always near
You're the sunshine to my day
I will never stay away
I love you, Mum, you're the best
Better than the rest.

Safiyah Iqbal

The Mum Store

Tall mums, short mums,
Always out of sort mums!
Big mums, thin mums,
Put it in the recycling bin! mums.
Strict mums, fun mums,
Relaxing under the sun mums.
Bad mums, good mums,
Eat healthy food mums.
Boring mums, joke mums,
"I only drink Diet Coke" mums.
Married mums, single mums,
Drop everything and mingle mums.
Lazy mums, working mums,
Tomboy mums, girly mums.
Always dancing and twirly mums
But of all these mums in the huge mum store
I love mine a lot, lot more!

Sophie Lily Kitson

What Is A Mummy?

A mummy is somebody
Who looks after you in
Your life. She is one of
Your important things in life.

She helps you find
Missing clothing,
Tidies your room,
Cooks delicious meals.

She takes you to school
In the morning and
Picks you up in the
Afternoon.

She is pleased when
You behave.
Angry when you
Misbehave.

Sometimes she can
Punish you but that's
Only because she loves
You and cares.

Sometimes when bad
Things happen she
Says it's okay even
Though she wants to cry.

Mwimba Marino

My Mum's The Best

My mum's the best!
She can obviously beat the rest
Surely my mum's the best
She can bake a real cake
While all the rest are fakes

She's the world's best mum
She just can't beat some
She can beat all
For her, that's as easy as rolling a ball

When your tummy rumbles
And all the other mums start to mumble
She makes you the best food
And because of that the other mums go in a bad mood

Thanks to her, my clothes are always neat
And in a show, she always saves me a seat
While all the other mums lie
I myself have got to go, so bye!

Zainab Sherif Mansour

My Mum

My mum is kind
My mum is amazing
My mum is why I am here and I would not be here without her

I don't know what I would do without her
She is my everything
She says to me goodnight when it is bedtime
Makes me happy when I am sad
And makes me delicious food

I love my mum so much and I will do forever
She is always in my heart
Always in my mind
And always there when I need her
She is my best friend.

I love you, Mum!

Alara Ela Kaya

Rohan's Mystery

I love you
You are my bestie
You are my mystery
You are a star in my sky
You are my eyes
You are my great assistant
You are my beating heart
I can't live without you
Love you, my mum.

Rohan Soultan

Blessing!

What a blessing a mother can be, a gift of love for eternity.
Every step of the way I go, I will always know that she'll be there for me.
A wise teacher to guide the way when all hope is lost.
A caring friend to share my success with,
And a knowledgeable doctor who will heal my pain.
You are one person, with so many roles
Yet you will always be my mother.
At last I have figured...
What a blessing my mother can be!

Sanaa Ali

What You Do For Me!

You do so much,
For me each day,
So I've decided I want to say,
Thank you,
For everything,
Each happy memory you bring.
All those times,
You played my game,
And were always there when I called your name.
Every act,
Of love and joy,
Every single book and toy,
You've bought for me,
With what you earn,
How you help me strive and learn.
I could go on,
For many days,
Talking about all the ways,
You make me feel,
When I'm with you,
I wish there was more I could do.
But is it okay,
If instead,
I write about what's in my head?
That you truly are,
As you can see,
The greatest mum there will ever be.

Zainab Imran (11)

The Best Mother

Oh, dear mother
I wouldn't want another
because you are very nice
and have lovely eyes.
Do you know why you're the best?
Because you always know the quest.
You are very good to me
and always have some tea.
You smell very well
and help me to spell.
When I feel sad
then you are not mad.
You are ever so kind
and never mind.
Then you say: "What's the matter?"
And make me feel better.
You also cook for us
and always take us to the bus.
It doesn't matter, we can play
on Sunday or any other day.
Now stop!
And give me a mop!
Let me help you
so I can show you
how much I love you.

Laura Jannova

Life's Too Short

Every day is a blessing,
Every day is another lucky day you get to enjoy.

Life is best served when you have a loving family,
When March rolls around, appreciate it.

Love life knowing your mam is always proud of the baby
she's created.

Laura Ridley (13)

World's Best Mum

Who's best and always there,
The one who's right and always fair,
The only one who cares,

Brightening up days,
With a jolly smile on her face,
Though every day's a maze,

Never a delay, always comes,
Smarter than them all, never dumb,
She's the world's best mum.

Sana Sahul Hameed

Happy Mother's Day, Nanna

Your smile met mine as I walked in,
You were always there for me.
You would be the one tidying up and throwing things in the
bin.
It was always like a dream, I was free.

When you talked, your voice was so comforting,
Like a bubble drifting on the breeze.
As the years flew by, I enjoyed the visits and your stories
were enchanting.
As I grew older, when I left you would give my hand a
squeeze.

You were so beautiful,
People wouldn't have guessed you were ill.
You were dealing with a bucket full,
You were so strong it gave me the chills.

You disappeared from our lives forever,
After that your smile never greeted us.
Without you here keeping us all together,
The first one without you there was such a fuss.

I wish you were here
To see the progress I am making at school.
It's crazy that in September I will be in the 9th year.
My friends are so understanding, they're cool.

Sometimes I see you,
It's like you're right in front of me.
I really miss you.

Ele Pike (13)

Heroes In My Heart

How shall I explain the love that's given?
For nothing is better than that received,
We always end by meeting in Heaven,
And for that we're gratefully relieved.

It is never enough to say thank you,
To Mother for giving us this dear life,
You support us in each step, till adieu,
God's gift to us all including top wife.

Thank you for bringing us to existence,
For working so hard to give us the best,
Which includes your own heartwarming presence,
Now it's my turn, Mum, to help let you rest.

As no man stands without such, to appear,
Mothers are our heroes, I hope that's clear.

Mary Ci Qi Tian

My Mum's The Best

Day and night
Night and day
You will guide me through the night
You will always be my light

Everyone will be sitting jealously
While we'll be sitting merrily
Me and you
You and me

My mum is really great
She's sweet as can be
When I need help I know
She's always there for me

Mum loves me all the time
Even when I'm a pest
She always takes good care of me
My mum's the best.

Cerys Jane Hubbard

My Mum

My mum is the best
Even though I can be a pest
She looks good in a T-shirt, trousers or dress
Her face is beautiful like a star
Shining bright, very far
I love my mum so much!

Neive Sarah Homewood

Mummy, My Hero

M ummy, you are so great!
U nique in many ways
M other's Day is a special day for a special mum
M y love to you
Y ou are my hero

M y beautiful mum, you'll never forget
Y ou are the best mum

H appy Mother's Day!
E very day I spend with you is brilliant
R oses, hearts and kisses
O nly you have the personality as a great mum.

Tayla Marie Woodham

Mother's Day Poem

Mother's Day, Mother's Day
What an extraordinary day!
Breakfast in bed hmm,

Toasted bread,
Singing in the street,
What a treat!
Children smiling,
While cuddling their mother,
Lovely gifts given,
Which is nice,
Wow, roasted chicken,
What good food given!
In the evening,
Happy dads kissing,
Mothers doing the same,
But doing it a bit more embarrassingly,
Mothers happily reading
The letters that are sent
But can smell flower scent
Happy families saying goodnight
Mother's Day, Mother's Day
What a happy day it was indeed.

Leon Zare

Marvellous Mother

She's always there with lots of care
She dresses us up and combs our hair
She always makes things fair and square
My mother's kind and really dear!

She's lots of fun, bright like the sun
She tells funny jokes and mummy puns
She doesn't care if we've lost or won
She'll still be there to cheer us on!

Her only limitation is her imagination
Mum is not only an inspiration
She is such a great fascination
This is without exaggeration!

Like Santa, she brings us presents in a great big sack
Great surprises to unpack and stack
Mum and we are like a pack
If we get lost, she can find our tracks
We love our mum to the moon and back!

"Where there's a will there's a way"
Mum's favourite quote still today
There's one more thing I want to say
So here's to you, happy Mother's Day!

**Joshua Babafunmilade &
Emmanuela Oluwafunmilola Oyeniyi**

My Mum

My mum is kind
She is like a diamond
She tucks me in bed at night
She is always right
She gives the best mummy cuddles
And lets me jump in puddles
She is the best to me
I love her, don't you see?

Marnee Robson

Mummy

You keep me safe when I am fearful
You wipe my eyes when I am tearful
You fill my days with colour and light
You cuddle with me in the night.

When things go wrong and out of hand
You never shout but understand
No matter what we go through
I will never stop loving you.

You make me happy, you're kind and funny
That is why I love you, Mummy
Thanks for every single day
So for this, happy Mother's Day.

Rebecca Skidmore (12)

To My Mom

It's Mother's Day
So I say:
Hip, hip, hooray!
On your day,
You don't lie.

"Thank you," I say,
I was born in May!
Ever since, you make me happy each day.
And I wish you would just stop, and lie,
On your day!

You keep wrong at bay,
So I can stay.
You still don't lie!
Now I've had my say:
Be happy today!

Zayan Ahmad Pannun

Mummy Is Great!

M ummy makes me feel better when I'm sad,
U nderneath her heart there is a treasure chest,
M uch love she has for her family,
M agic sparkles in her hair,
Y et she still cleans up my mess!

I like it when she reads my bedtime story,
S he always helps me when I'm stuck,

G enerously, she gives me hugs and kisses,
R eliably, she is there when I need her,
E very time I wake up, she is there for me,
A lways, she looks after me as well as she can,
T he most special thing about her is that I love her too!

Megan North

My Mum

My mum is a loyal, thoughtful friend
Who is always by my side
When I'm down or disheartened
She cheers me up.

My mum is a creative thinker,
An artist and a baker
Who makes scrumptious cakes
The cuisines created by her are magnificent to devour.

My mum is a fine-fingered, hardworking woman
Cooking, sorting laundry,
Looking after us rambunctious children
And looking after Dad.
What could I do without my mum?

Thank you.
It may be small words
But from me it means a lot from the heart

I would be a completely down, struggling person without
your support
So please treasure this poem like I adore you
And have a lovely Mother's Day.

Haniya Hanif

The Best Mum

My mum is the best cook
Because she's the best mum ever
My mum is kind
She's the role model
She's my mum
And she's the best.

Chester Maldutis

A Little Appreciation

Gentle taps on grumpy doors every time the morning calls,
Then shouts up the stairs for tea every night.
Every bit of clothing put away in tidy drawers
And you pretend you don't feel guilty that you piled it on
your chair in a messy heap.

Every time she was your personal taxi driver
Every rushing-in-and-out to this and that and there.
Every time she caught you when you fell through teenage
traps
And brought you back to the person she knew you were.

Every time she gave solutions to impossible answers,
An all-knowing goddess you worshipped in your youth
And you detested in your adolescence because,
yes, Mother knows best.

Every trip abroad when you saw her in strangers' faces
Every one of her colleagues saying, "So she's your mum!
Lucky you!"
Every time you cried and she made it all a joke
Every job you failed, every relationship that fell through.

Every time you meet her now
The kids are too much for you to take
But she does it easily and you don't know how
She smiles, hugs you and lets you escape.

Every time she fades away, a little more every day
And you fear the moment she's completely gone
Because she held the world together from the moment you
began

Frozen with fear, but warm inside
Because you know she's still there
Telling you to get dressed
Go out and see the world
And that she's with you to see it too.
Your rock in life and death.
Mother knows best.

Rosina Catrin Jones

My Mum

When I'm scared
You're there.
When I'm sad
You're there.
When I cry
You hold me close
And wipe those tears away.
This is a thank you note
Thank you.
You I love the most
And best of all
You're my mum.

Jonny Neill

Mum

Mum, Mum, she doesn't like rum
Her cakes are the best
But she barely ever rests
She likes to read
But doesn't feel the need
As lovely as the Queen
And never mean
As sweet as a flower
I only wish she had a superpower
Always kind
She binds our family together
She always finds time to love and care
I love my mum.

Freya Myrron Mackay

My Mum Is...

My mum is awesome
My mum is great
I love her more, she loves me more
When I stare at the moon it reminds me of her
She loves wearing yellow and it suits her
Everybody likes it
Reminds me of the sun and mustard
And the best mum I ever had
In years I will remember the best times we had
I could never be sad
Happy Mother's Day, Mum.

Albert Stanley Unsworth-Rojas (14)

To The Greatest Mum In The World

To the one that fed me until I got filled
To the one that protected me like a shield
To the one who helped me form what I have become
To the one who stayed by me when I was sick
To the one that did not let me get hurt until I was big
To the one who sacrificed her dreams for me
I love you, Mum.

Tahmeed Mahdi Kabir

My Best Mum

My mum is the best for me,
She understands me better,
She enjoys me being me,
She is enough for me,
She makes me feel me,

Kind and generous describes my mum,
She is my comfort and support during hard times,
I give her hard times sometimes, but she still smiles,
She is strong with a heart as soft as wool,

My mum is all I need,
She teaches me and never fails me,
She reminds me to never give up because I am still learning,
She corrects me, and praises me,
She guides me only to the right direction,
I love you, Mum, simply because you are my mum.

Brianna Tanya Musengeyi

My Special Mum

My mum is the best one for me,
She supports me when I need it,
She is happy when I am happy,
She cares for me when I am ill,
She still loves me even when she is angry with me,
And she is my mum,

My mum never doubts me even when I am wrong,
She is my special friend who never judges me,
She helps me to improve in everything,
She still trusts me when I am either naughty or not,
And she is my mum,

My mum is not perfect and that you agree
To me my mum is so close to perfect,
She is kind and forgiving,
My mum is trustworthy,
My mum makes mistakes and it is fine with me,
She is the best,
And she is my mum,

My mum teaches me how to love,
She is there for the whole family,
With family around, my mum feels whole,
My mum lives and works for the whole family,
Guess what? My mum never complains,
She is so sweet, she is so sweet,
And she is my mum.

Danielle Rumbidzo Musengeyi

I Love You, Mum

I love you because we have so much fun
I'm glad that I'm your special one.
I love you because you show me the way
You're here to help me every day.
I love you because you're always near
I feel safe when you are here.
I love you because when we go exploring
It is fun and exciting and never boring.
I love you because no matter where I play
You're never, ever far away.
I love you because you make me giggle
You tickle and tickle until you make me giggle.
I love you because you hold me tight
And keep me warm and safe through the night.
But the biggest reason for loving you
Is that I know in my heart you love me too.

Joe Squire

My Wonderful Mum

M um, you really are so smart,
O h and also you have a loving heart,
T o clean up and tidy all day! Well...
H eroic mum is here, hooray!
E mpathetic, amazing, wonderful and
R eally helpful, you'll always have a plan,
S o, Mum, this day is for you,

D on't stress, relax. I'll clean up too,
A nd I hope you know that I love you so,
Y ou are the best mum I'll ever know!

Siena-Maria Dixon

My Mother

Mothers come in all shapes and sizes,
There are tall ones and short ones,
Thin ones and fat ones,
There are loud ones and quiet ones,
Silly ones and serious ones,
Of course, there is my mum!

Born in the spring of '82,
Came a little girl, fresh and new.
She giggled,
She laughed and started to cry.
So her mum sang her a lullaby.

So, years into the future,
In 1985, she got a brother,
Full of life.
Lots of years passed and...

Then, after years in Gran Canaria,
She came home and settled down,
Started a family... this is where I come in!
She found a boyfriend,
Tall, dark and mysterious,
And suddenly they shared a flat,
Then I arrived, quick as a bat!

Years flew by and I grew older,
I got braver, I got bolder,
At the age of four, I got a little fright,
Whilst the lady's clothes got tight.

She was having a baby,
A tiny little boy,
He was small and wriggly,
Nothing like a toy.

Now she sits in front of me,
A woman tall and proud,
The woman is my mother.
And this is her tale,
Very much abridged,
But this is still my mother,
And sometimes I wonder,
Does she know how much I love her?

Ruby Eames

My Mother

Meal-maker
Love-bringer
Dust-taker
Time-giver
Car-driver
Life-bringer
Happiness-giver
Restaurant-payer
Homework-helper
Cuddle-creator
Tear-cleaner
Kind listener
Put them all together,
You're my mother!

Clara Gillard

Our Superlative Mother

Our mothers care for us,
But we care way more!
Some of our mothers fuss,
Because they might be poor!
They will always be by our side,
But we still need to show respect back to them.
When we were little they sometimes were like a very joyful ride!
When we get older we might think they are dumb!
But listen to this, they are not.
Our mothers do all the housework.
You might sometimes even feel that our love might be a massive knot.
Did you know that we all think that our mothers aren't a jerk?
We all know that we always can't be together,
But for now we are.
We can now play whenever we want in this fair weather.
Our mothers have always helped us when we get our scars.
Our mothers are our life,
They are our heart,
They are our mothers,
They are our superheroes!

Varshaa Eelakesan

M.O.M. - Most Outstanding Mom

Dear Mom, you are the best,
I think you are awesome, you know the rest,
Even though we sometimes fight,
You have always got my best interests in sight,
You work so hard day in day out,
You deserve a big shout out,
Working almost every day,
What you need is a holiday,
I ought to say this much more often,
You are the best, not at all rotten,
To end this poem with sparkle, dazzle and fizz,
You are brilliant, Mom, a real whizz,
You definitely deserve to know this,
Because you are my mom, the most outstanding mother.

Hermione Mekonnen

Beloved Mother

My mother is the best,
As she is always there for me,
Her footsteps are my destiny.
She's sweeter than a peach,
I love her beyond reach.
My mum, how early she wakes,
To make delicious bakes.
She cares for me with all her heart,
She seems to think I'm very smart.
My mum is mine,
And with that I'm fine.
Just fine.

Maya Aleksandra Tinney

My Mum

My mum is very smart
And she always plays her part
Whenever I frown
She always turns it upside down
Her smile is bright
She doesn't put up a fight
And that's why I love her
She is so beautiful
And walks and talks so graceful.

Ara Kayode

Mum, You Are The Best

Mum, you are the best,
And no one can protest.
You will always believe in me,
And because of that,
I'll get a good degree.

Mum, you are the best,
Because of you, I am so blessed
You will always love,
Just like a white dove.

I wish you a happy Mother's Day,
We'll love each other all that way!
I will love you with all my heart,
It was you who made me smart!

I will love you more than anyone,
You are the best thing my dad won!
I hope you have a brilliant day for mothers
And you are way better than the others!

Michael Jackauskas

My Mum

I love my mum more than my imaginary brother
She's really nice and doesn't make me pay the price
A wonderful mum she is even though she drinks fizz
Mum is the best who likes to jest
A really good cook who likes to rub my tummy
I call her miraculous, our big ray of sunshine
Talented and excellent
Guess what?
I love my mum!

Angel Wale-Akinlua (11)

My Mummy

My mummy has blonde hair
My mummy has hazel eyes
My mummy loves pink
My mummy is beautiful
My mummy is kind
She loves everyone
And she is called Michelle
I love you, Mum.

Lily Grace Brown

Nano

I remember when I used to go
To a flat in a placid neighbourhood,
A pretty place, where a blossom tree grows
And the grass bristled where it stood.

Inside that flat was someone,
Someone very special to me,
Someone who I'll always love a ton,
Someone who's now flying free.

That someone is my Nano,
Whom I still adore,
Though her life is sadly no more,
She'll be forever cared for.

An angel in the sky,
A treasured gift to the world above,
I didn't want to say goodbye,
But I'll remember her with love.

Nowadays, I tend to go,
To her final resting place,
A precious place, where a large tree grows
And the flowers twirl with grace...

Zara Siddiqui

Mother

M um, you really do mean the whole world to me...

O ur connection is like superglue, we need our mums...

T he love between us really means we fit perfectly...

H ard-working, individual mums provide everything for you...

E verlasting love is like walking on a tightrope till 3011...

R espect your mums for everything! They love you and you love them.

Ella Nicole Williams

Mum

I am lucky to have a friend like you
You raise my spirits when I am blue
You shine like the sun
And you are really, really fun
I am glad you are my mum.

Iqra Jawaid

Mama, I Love You!

I love my mum
She's the best mum in the world
My mum is really nice because
She always puts me in bed
And reads me stories too
Together we make lovely memories
And also go to lots of lovely places
Like the time we went to Paris
And the time we went to the festival in Cyprus
Also, if I could choose any mum in the world
I would choose mine
I love her and she loves me
We're the perfect match.

Sienna Lily Jamieson

Mum

I think my mum is the best
I think she is better than the rest
She does so many things for me
It makes me as happy as can be
She is the best ever
I know I will love her forever.

Alice Lilian McDonnell

World's Best Mum

My mum is the best
Better than the rest
She plays with me every day
And teaches me how to pray.

My mum is the best
She is a treasure chest
My mum is great after all
Not a bull.

My mum is the best,
Did she get a rest?
I love you, Mum
Here I come.

Her favourite colour is red
She helps me when I hurt my head
All the time she's there she cares

She is very kind
One of a kind
I love my mum!

Abigail Ceri Appleton (8)

Young Writers Information

We hope you have enjoyed reading this book – and that you will continue to in the coming years.

If you're a young writer who enjoys reading and creative writing, or the parent of an enthusiastic poet or story writer, do visit our website www.youngwriters.co.uk. Here you will find free competitions, workshops and games, as well as recommended reads, a poetry glossary and our blog.

If you would like to order further copies of this book, or any of our other titles give us a call or visit www.youngwriters.co.uk.

Young Writers
Remus House
Coltsfoot Drive
Peterborough
PE2 9BF

(01733) 890066
info@youngwriters.co.uk